TAO TE CHING

道德經

Ultimate Bilingual Edition (4-in-1)

English · Traditional Chinese · Simplified Chinese · Ancient Seal Script

LAO TZU

Published by Jade Ink Press

First Edition: February 2025
Printed in the United States of America

CONTENTS

ABOUT THIS EDITION

Welcome to a unique journey through the "Tao Te Ching," presented in four different forms of writing that span the centuries. This edition lets you experience Lao Tzu's timeless wisdom through multiple lenses - from ancient script to modern text, from Chinese to English.

Each chapter opens to a two-page layout. On the left, you'll find Traditional Chinese characters above Simplified Chinese. On the right, James Legge's English translation appears above the Small Seal Script.

We've chosen James Legge's 1891 translation for good reason. As one of the first Western scholars to master Classical Chinese, Legge created a translation that strikes a perfect balance - it's precise enough for scholarly study yet clear enough for everyday reading. His careful attention to the original text's meaning shines through in straightforward, accessible English that still resonates today.

Here's something fascinating: archaeological discoveries, particularly the Ma-wang-tui silk texts (168 B.C.) show that the original "Tao Te Ching" actually began with what we now call the Te Ching (chapters 38-81), followed by the Tao Ching (chapters 1-37). While we've maintained the conventional chapter order familiar to most readers, this archaeological finding offers an intriguing glimpse into the text's early history.

The Traditional Chinese text is arranged from left to right and top to bottom, following modern reading conventions. Modern punctuation marks appear in the text to enhance readability, though such marks didn't exist in ancient times. The Simplified Chinese version shows the form commonly used in mainland

China today.

At the bottom of the right page, you'll find the Small Seal Script in its traditional right-to-left, top-to-bottom order without punctuation. Since Lao Tzu lived around the 6th century B.C. - about 300 years before Small Seal Script was standardized by Ch'in Shih-huang-ti - he would have used an even earlier form of writing. However, we've included Small Seal Script because it gives us a fascinating glimpse into how Chinese writing evolved, bridging the gap between ancient and modern forms.

In this edition, we focus on presenting the core text of the "Tao Te Ching" without additional commentary, allowing readers to engage directly with these profound teachings through multiple perspectives. Whether you're a student of Chinese philosophy, a language enthusiast, or simply drawn to ancient wisdom, we hope this four-script edition enriches your understanding and appreciation of this remarkable work.

第一章

　　道可道，非常道。名可名，非常名。無名天地之始，有名萬物之母。故常無欲，以觀其妙;常有欲，以觀其徼。此兩者同出而異名,同謂之玄,玄之又玄，眾妙之門。

第一章

　　道可道，非常道。名可名，非常名。无名天地之始，有名万物之母。故常无欲，以观其妙;常有欲，以观其徼。此两者同出而异名,同谓之玄,玄之又玄，众妙之门。

I

The Tao that can be trodden is not the enduring and unchanging Tao. The name that can be named is not the enduring and unchanging name.

(Conceived of as) having no name, it is the Originator of heaven and earth; (conceived of as) having a name, it is the Mother of all things.

Always without desire we must be found,
If its deep mystery we would sound;
But if desire always within us be,
Its outer fringe is all that we shall see.

Under these two aspects, it is really the same; but as development takes place, it receives the different names. Together we call them the Mystery. Where the Mystery is the deepest is the gate of all that is subtle and wonderful.

SEAL SCRIPT

第二章

天下皆知美之為美，斯惡已。皆知善之為善，斯不善已。故有無相生，難易相成，長短相較，高下相傾,音聲相和,前後相隨。是以聖人處無為之事,行不言之教;萬物作焉而不辭, 生而不有, 為而不恃,功成而弗居。夫唯弗居，是以不去。

第二章

天下皆知美之为美，斯恶已。皆知善之为善，斯不善已。故有无相生，难易相成，长短相较，高下相倾,音声相和,前后相随。是以圣人处无为之事,行不言之教;万物作焉而不辞, 生而不有, 为而不恃,功成而弗居。夫唯弗居，是以不去。

II

All in the world know the beauty of the beautiful, and in doing this they have (the idea of) what ugliness is; they all know the skill of the skilful, and in doing this they have (the idea of) what the want of skill is.

So it is that existence and non-existence give birth the one to (the idea of) the other; that difficulty and ease produce the one (the idea of) the other; that length and shortness fashion out the one the figure of the other; that (the ideas of) height and lowness arise from the contrast of the one with the other; that the musical notes and tones become harmonious through the relation of one with another; and that being before and behind give the idea of one following another.

Therefore the sage manages affairs without doing anything, and conveys his instructions without the use of speech.

All things spring up, and there is not one which declines to show itself; they grow, and there is no claim made for their ownership; they go through their processes, and there is no expectation (of a reward for the results). The work is accomplished, and there is no resting in it (as an achievement).

The work is done, but how no one can see;
'Tis this that makes the power not cease to be.

SEAL SCRIPT

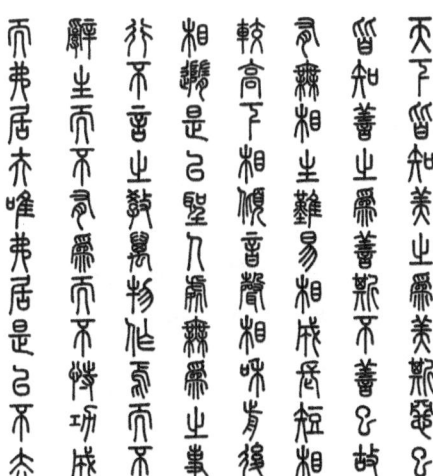

9

第三章

　　不尚賢，使民不爭；不貴難得之貨，使民不為盜;不見可欲，使民心不亂。是以聖人之治，虛其心，實其腹，弱其志，強其骨。常使民無知無欲。使夫智者不敢為也。為無為，則無不治。

第三章

　　不尚贤，使民不争；不贵难得之货，使民不为盗;不见可欲，使民心不乱。是以圣人之治，虚其心，实其腹，弱其志，强其骨。常使民无知无欲。使夫智者不敢为也。为无为，则无不治。

III

Not to value and employ men of superior ability is the way to keep the people from rivalry among themselves; not to prize articles which are difficult to procure is the way to keep them from becoming thieves; not to show them what is likely to excite their desires is the way to keep their minds from disorder.

Therefore the sage, in the exercise of his government, empties their minds, fills their bellies, weakens their wills, and strengthens their bones.

He constantly (tries to) keep them without knowledge and without desire, and where there are those who have knowledge, to keep them from presuming to act (on it). When there is this abstinence from action, good order is universal.

SEAL SCRIPT

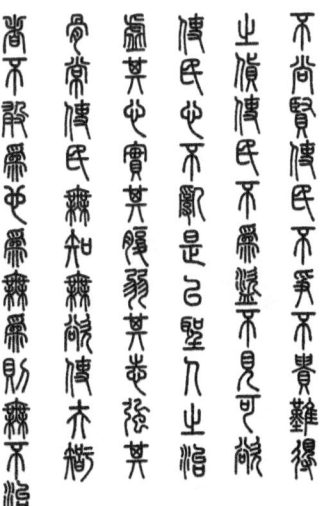

第四章

　　道沖而用之或不盈，淵兮似萬物之宗；挫其銳，解其紛，和其光，同其塵，湛兮似或存。吾不知誰之子，象帝之先。

第四章

　　道冲而用之或不盈，渊兮似万物之宗；挫其锐，解其纷，和其光，同其尘，湛兮似或存。吾不知谁之子，象帝之先。

IV

The Tao is (like) the emptiness of a vessel; and in our employment of it we must be on our guard against all fulness. How deep and unfathomable it is, as if it were the Honoured Ancestor of all things!

We should blunt our sharp points, and unravel the complications of things; we should attemper our brightness, and bring ourselves into agreement with the obscurity of others. How pure and still the Tao is, as if it would ever so continue!

I do not know whose son it is. It might appear to have been before God.

SEAL SCRIPT

第五章

　　天地不仁，以萬物為芻狗；聖人不仁，以百姓為芻狗。天地之間，其猶橐籥乎?虛而不屈，動而愈出。多言數窮，不如守中。

第五章

　　天地不仁，以万物为刍狗；圣人不仁，以百姓为刍狗。天地之间，其犹橐籥乎?虚而不屈，动而愈出。多言数穷，不如守中。

V

Heaven and earth do not act from (the impulse of) any wish to be benevolent; they deal with all things as the dogs of grass are dealt with. The sages do not act from (any wish to be) benevolent; they deal with the people as the dogs of grass are dealt with.

May not the space between heaven and earth be compared to a bellows?

'Tis emptied, yet it loses not its power;
'Tis moved again, and sends forth air the more.
Much speech to swift exhaustion lead we see;
Your inner being guard, and keep it free.

SEAL SCRIPT

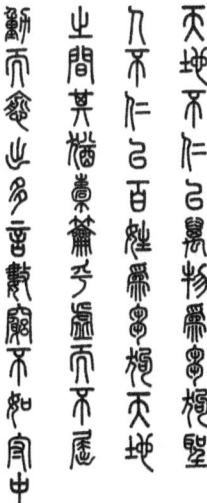

第六章

谷神不死，是謂玄牝。玄牝之門，是謂天地根。綿綿若存，用之不勤。

第六章

谷神不死，是谓玄牝。玄牝之门，是谓天地根。绵绵若存，用之不勤。

VI

The valley spirit dies not, aye the same;
The female mystery thus do we name.
Its gate, from which at first they issued forth,
Is called the root from which grew heaven and earth.
Long and unbroken does its power remain,
Used gently, and without the touch of pain.

SEAL SCRIPT

第七章

天長地久。天地所以能長且久者，以其不自生，
故能長生。是以聖人後其身而身先；外其身而身存。
非以其無私邪，故能成其私。

第七章

天长地久。天地所以能长且久者，以其不自生，
故能长生。是以圣人后其身而身先；外其身而身存。
非以其无私邪，故能成其私。

VII

Heaven is long-enduring and earth continues long. The reason why heaven and earth are able to endure and continue thus long is because they do not live of, or for, themselves. This is how they are able to continue and endure.

Therefore the sage puts his own person last, and yet it is found in the foremost place; he treats his person as if it were foreign to him, and yet that person is preserved. Is it not because he has no personal and private ends, that therefore such ends are realised?

SEAL SCRIPT

第八章

上善若水。水善利萬物而不爭，處眾人之所惡，故幾於道。居善地，心善淵，與善仁，言善信，正善治，事善能，動善時。夫唯不爭，故無尤。

第八章

上善若水。水善利万物而不争，处众人之所恶，故几于道。居善地，心善渊，与善仁，言善信，正善治，事善能，动善时。夫唯不争，故无尤。

VIII

The highest excellence is like (that of) water. The excellence of water appears in its benefiting all things, and in its occupying, without striving (to the contrary), the low place which all men dislike. Hence (its way) is near to (that of) the Tao.

The excellence of a residence is in (the suitability of) the place; that of the mind is in abysmal stillness; that of associations is in their being with the virtuous; that of government is in its securing good order; that of (the conduct of) affairs is in its ability; and that of (the initiation of) any movement is in its timeliness.

And when (one with the highest excellence) does not wrangle (about his low position), no one finds fault with him.

SEAL SCRIPT

第九章

　　持而盈之，不如其已；揣而梲之，不可長保。金玉滿堂，莫之能守；富貴而驕，自遺其咎。功成身退，天之道也。

第九章

　　持而盈之，不如其已；揣而棁之，不可长保。金玉满堂，莫之能守；富贵而骄，自遗其咎。功成身退，天之道也。

IX

It is better to leave a vessel unfilled, than to attempt to carry it when it is full. If you keep feeling a point that has been sharpened, the point cannot long preserve its sharpness.

When gold and jade fill the hall, their possessor cannot keep them safe. When wealth and honours lead to arrogancy, this brings its evil on itself. When the work is done, and one's name is becoming distinguished, to withdraw into obscurity is the way of Heaven.

SEAL SCRIPT

第十章

載營魄抱一，能無離乎?專氣致柔，能嬰兒乎?滌除玄覽，能無疵乎?愛國治民，能無知乎?天門開闔，能為雌乎?明白四達，能無為乎?生之，畜之。生而不有，為而不恃，長而不宰，是謂玄德。

第十章

載营魄抱一，能无离乎?专气致柔，能婴儿乎?涤除玄览，能无疵乎?爱国治民，能无知乎?天门开阖，能为雌乎?明白四达，能无为乎?生之，畜之。生而不有，为而不恃，长而不宰，是谓玄德。

X

When the intelligent and animal souls are held together in one embrace, they can be kept from separating. When one gives undivided attention to the (vital) breath, and brings it to the utmost degree of pliancy, he can become as a (tender) babe. When he has cleansed away the most mysterious sights (of his imagination), he can become without a flaw.

In loving the people and ruling the state, cannot he proceed without any (purpose of) action? In the opening and shutting of his gates of heaven, cannot he do so as a female bird? While his intelligence reaches in every direction, cannot he (appear to) be without knowledge?

(The Tao) produces (all things) and nourishes them; it produces them and does not claim them as its own; it does all, and yet does not boast of it; it presides over all, and yet does not control them. This is what is called 'The mysterious Quality' (of the Tao).

SEAL SCRIPT

25

第十一章

三十輻，共一轂，當其無，有車之用。埏埴以為器，當其無，有器之用。鑿戶牖以為室，當其無，有室之用。故有之以為利，無之以為用。

第十一章

三十辐，共一毂，当其无，有车之用。埏埴以为器，当其无，有器之用。凿户牖以为室，当其无，有室之用。故有之以为利，无之以为用。

XI

The thirty spokes unite in the one nave; but it is on the empty space (for the axle), that the use of the wheel depends. Clay is fashioned into vessels; but it is on their empty hollowness, that their use depends. The door and windows are cut out (from the walls) to form an apartment; but it is on the empty space (within), that its use depends. Therefore, what has a (positive) existence serves for profitable adaptation, and what has not that for (actual) usefulness.

SEAL SCRIPT

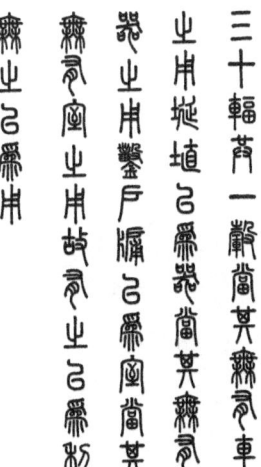

第十二章

五色令人目盲，五音令人耳聾，五味令人口爽，馳騁畋獵令人心發狂，難得之貨令人行妨。是以聖人為腹不為目，故去彼取此。

第十二章

五色令人目盲，五音令人耳聋，五味令人口爽，驰骋畋猎令人心发狂，难得之货令人行妨。是以圣人为腹不为目，故去彼取此。

XII

Colour's five hues from th' eyes their sight will take;
Music's five notes the ears as deaf can make;
The flavours five deprive the mouth of taste;
The chariot course, and the wild hunting waste
Make mad the mind; and objects rare and strange,
Sought for, men's conduct will to evil change.

Therefore the sage seeks to satisfy (the craving of) the belly, and not the (insatiable longing of the) eyes. He puts from him the latter, and prefers to seek the former.

SEAL SCRIPT

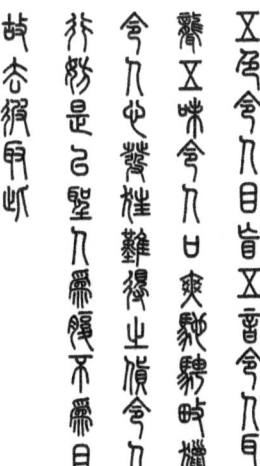

第十三章

寵辱若驚,貴大患若身。何謂寵辱若驚?寵為下,得之若驚,失之若驚,是謂寵辱若驚。何謂貴大患若身?吾所以有大患者,為吾有身,及吾無身,吾有何患?故貴以身為天下,若可寄天下;愛以身為天下,若可托天下。

第十三章

宠辱若惊,贵大患若身。何谓宠辱若惊?宠为下,得之若惊,失之若惊,是谓宠辱若惊。何谓贵大患若身?吾所以有大患者,为吾有身,及吾无身,吾有何患?故贵以身为天下,若可寄天下;爱以身为天下,若可托天下。

XIII

Favour and disgrace would seem equally to be feared; honour and great calamity, to be regarded as personal conditions (of the same kind).

What is meant by speaking thus of favour and disgrace? Disgrace is being in a low position (after the enjoyment of favour). The getting that (favour) leads to the apprehension (of losing it), and the losing it leads to the fear of (still greater calamity):—this is what is meant by saying that favour and disgrace would seem equally to be feared.

And what is meant by saying that honour and great calamity are to be (similarly) regarded as personal conditions? What makes me liable to great calamity is my having the body (which I call myself); if I had not the body, what great calamity could come to me?

Therefore he who would administer the kingdom, honouring it as he honours his own person, may be employed to govern it, and he who would administer it with the love which he bears to his own person may be entrusted with it.

SEAL SCRIPT

第十四章

視之不見名曰夷，聽之不聞名曰希，搏之不得名曰微。此三者不可致詰，故混而為一。其上不皦，其下不昧。繩繩不可名，復歸於無物。是謂無狀之狀，無物之象，是謂惚恍。迎之不見其首，隨之不見其後。執古之道，以御今之有。能知古始，是謂道紀。

第十四章

視之不见名曰夷，听之不闻名曰希，搏之不得名曰微。此三者不可致诘，故混而为一。其上不皦，其下不昧。绳绳不可名，复归于无物。是谓无状之状，无物之象，是谓惚恍。迎之不见其首，随之不见其后。执古之道，以御今之有。能知古始，是谓道纪。

XIV

We look at it, and we do not see it, and we name it 'the Equable.' We listen to it, and we do not hear it, and we name it 'the Inaudible.' We try to grasp it, and do not get hold of it, and we name it 'the Subtle.' With these three qualities, it cannot be made the subject of description; and hence we blend them together and obtain The One.

Its upper part is not bright, and its lower part is not obscure. Ceaseless in its action, it yet cannot be named, and then it again returns and becomes nothing. This is called the Form of the Formless, and the Semblance of the Invisible; this is called the Fleeting and Indeterminable.

We meet it and do not see its Front; we follow it, and do not see its Back. When we can lay hold of the Tao of old to direct the things of the present day, and are able to know it as it was of old in the beginning, this is called (unwinding) the clue of Tao.

SEAL SCRIPT

第十五章

古之善為士者，微妙玄通，深不可識。夫唯不可識，故強為之容:豫兮若冬涉川，猶兮若畏四鄰，儼兮其若客，渙兮若冰之將釋，敦兮其若樸，曠兮其若谷，渾兮其若濁。孰能濁以靜之徐清?孰能安以久動之徐生?保此道者不欲盈，夫唯不盈，故能蔽不新成。

第十五章

古之善为士者，微妙玄通，深不可识。夫唯不可识，故强为之容:豫兮若冬涉川，犹兮若畏四邻，俨兮其若客，涣兮若冰之将释，敦兮其若朴，旷兮其若谷，浑兮其若浊。孰能浊以静之徐清?孰能安以久动之徐生?保此道者不欲盈，夫唯不盈，故能蔽不新成。

XV

The skilful masters (of the Tao) in old times, with a subtle and exquisite penetration, comprehended its mysteries, and were deep (also) so as to elude men's knowledge. As they were thus beyond men's knowledge, I will make an effort to describe of what sort they appeared to be.

Shrinking looked they like those who wade through a stream in winter; ir-resolute like those who are afraid of all around them; grave like a guest (in awe of his host); evanescent like ice that is melting away; unpretentious like wood that has not been fashioned into anything; vacant like a valley, and dull like muddy water.

Who can (make) the muddy water (clear)? Let it be still, and it will gradual-ly become clear. Who can secure the condition of rest? Let movement go on, and the condition of rest will gradually arise.

They who preserve this method of the Tao do not wish to be full (of them-selves). It is through their not being full of themselves that they can afford to seem worn and not appear new and complete.

SEAL SCRIPT

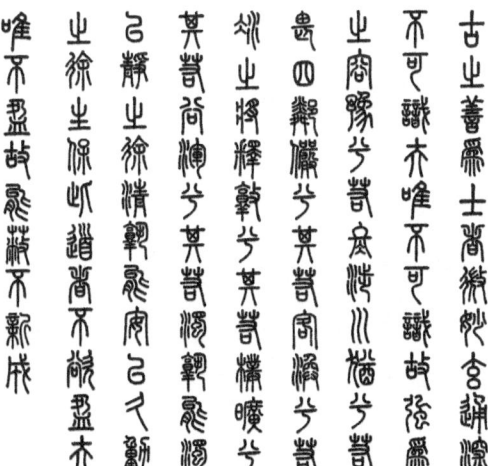

第十六章

致虛極，守靜篤。萬物並作，吾以觀復。夫物芸芸，各復歸其根。歸根曰靜，是曰復命。復命曰常，知常曰明。不知常，妄作凶。知常容，容乃公，公乃王，王乃天，天乃道，道乃久，沒身不殆。

第十六章

致虚极，守静笃。万物并作，吾以观复。夫物芸芸，各复归其根。归根曰静，是曰复命。复命曰常，知常曰明。不知常，妄作凶。知常容，容乃公，公乃王，王乃天，天乃道，道乃久，没身不殆。

XVI

The (state of) vacancy should be brought to the utmost degree, and that of stillness guarded with unwearying vigour. All things alike go through their processes of activity, and (then) we see them return (to their original state). When things (in the vegetable world) have displayed their luxuriant growth, we see each of them return to its root. This returning to their root is what we call the state of stillness; and that stillness may be called a reporting that they have fulfilled their appointed end.

The report of that fulfilment is the regular, unchanging rule. To know that unchanging rule is to be intelligent; not to know it leads to wild movements and evil issues. The knowledge of that unchanging rule produces a (grand) capacity and forbearance, and that capacity and forbearance lead to a community (of feeling with all things). From this community of feeling comes a kingliness of character; and he who is king-like goes on to be heaven-like. In that likeness to heaven he possesses the Tao. Possessed of the Tao, he endures long; and to the end of his bodily life, is exempt from all danger of decay.

SEAL SCRIPT

37

第十七章

太上，下知有之，其次親而譽之，其次畏之，其次侮之。信不足焉，有不信焉。悠兮其貴言，功成事遂，百姓皆謂我自然。

第十七章

太上，下知有之，其次亲而誉之，其次畏之，其次侮之。信不足焉，有不信焉。悠兮其贵言，功成事遂，百姓皆谓我自然。

XVII

In the highest antiquity, (the people) did not know that there were (their rulers). In the next age they loved them and praised them. In the next they feared them; in the next they despised them. Thus it was that when faith (in the Tao) was deficient (in the rulers) a want of faith in them ensued (in the people).

How irresolute did those (earliest rulers) appear, showing (by their reticence) the importance which they set upon their words! Their work was done and their undertakings were successful, while the people all said, 'We are as we are, of ourselves!'

SEAL SCRIPT

第十八章

大道廢，有仁義；智慧出，有大偽；六親不和，有孝慈；國家昏亂，有忠臣。

第十八章

大道废，有仁义；智慧出，有大伪；六亲不和，有孝慈；国家昏乱，有忠臣。

XVIII

When the Great Tao (Way or Method) ceased to be observed, benevolence and righteousness came into vogue. (Then) appeared wisdom and shrewdness, and there ensued great hypocrisy.

When harmony no longer prevailed throughout the six kinships, filial sons found their manifestation; when the states and clans fell into disorder, loyal ministers appeared.

SEAL SCRIPT

第十九章

絕聖棄智，民利百倍；絕仁棄義，民復孝慈；絕巧棄利，盜賊無有。此三者以為文不足，故令有所屬:見素抱樸，少私寡欲。

第十九章

绝圣弃智，民利百倍；绝仁弃义，民复孝慈；绝巧弃利，盗贼无有。此三者以为文不足，故令有所属:见素抱朴，少私寡欲。

XIX

If we could renounce our sageness and discard our wisdom, it would be better for the people a hundredfold. If we could renounce our benevolence and discard our righteousness, the people would again become filial and kindly. If we could renounce our artful contrivances and discard our (scheming for) gain, there would be no thieves nor robbers.

> Those three methods (of government)
> Thought olden ways in elegance did fail
> And made these names their want of worth to veil;
> But simple views, and courses plain and true
> Would selfish ends and many lusts eschew.

SEAL SCRIPT

43

第二十章

絕學無憂，唯之與阿，相去幾何?善之與惡，相去若何?人之所畏，不可不畏。荒兮其未央哉!眾人熙熙，如享太牢，如春登台。我獨泊兮，其未兆，如嬰兒之未孩；儡儡兮，若無所歸。眾人皆有餘，而我獨若遺。我愚人之心也哉!沌沌兮，俗人昭昭，我獨若昏。俗人察察，我獨悶悶。澹兮其若海，飂兮若無止。眾人皆有以,而我獨頑似鄙。我獨異於人，而貴食母。

第二十章

绝学无忧，唯之与阿，相去几何?善之与恶，相去若何?人之所畏，不可不畏。荒兮其未央哉!众人熙熙，如享太牢，如春登台。我独泊兮，其未兆，如婴儿之未孩；儡儡兮，若无所归。众人皆有余，而我独若遗。我愚人之心也哉!沌沌兮，俗人昭昭，我独若昏。俗人察察，我独闷闷。澹兮其若海，飂兮若无止。众人皆有以,而我独顽似鄙。我独异于人，而贵食母。

XX

When we renounce learning we have no troubles.
The (ready) 'yes,' and (flattering) 'yea;'—
Small is the difference they display.
But mark their issues, good and ill;—
What space the gulf between shall fill?

What all men fear is indeed to be feared; but how wide and without end is the range of questions (asking to be discussed)!

The multitude of men look satisfied and pleased; as if enjoying a full banquet, as if mounted on a tower in spring. I alone seem listless and still, my desires having as yet given no indication of their presence. I am like an infant which has not yet smiled. I look dejected and forlorn, as if I had no home to go to. The multitude of men all have enough and to spare. I alone seem to have lost everything. My mind is that of a stupid man; I am in a state of chaos.

Ordinary men look bright and intelligent, while I alone seem to be benighted. They look full of discrimination, while I alone am dull and confused. I seem to be carried about as on the sea, drifting as if I had nowhere to rest. All men have their spheres of action, while I alone seem dull and incapable, like a rude borderer. (Thus) I alone am different from other men, but I value the nursing-mother (the Tao).

SEAL SCRIPT

45

第二十一章

孔德之容，惟道是從。道之為物，惟恍惟惚。惚兮恍兮,其中有象;恍兮惚兮,其中有物。窈兮冥兮,其中有精;其精甚真,其中有信。自今及古,其名不去,以閱眾甫。吾何以知眾甫之狀哉?以此。

第二十一章

孔德之容，惟道是从。道之为物，惟恍惟惚。惚兮恍兮,其中有象;恍兮惚兮,其中有物。窈兮冥兮,其中有精;其精甚真,其中有信。自今及古,其名不去,以阅众甫。吾何以知众甫之状哉?以此。

XXI

The grandest forms of active force
From Tao come, their only source.
Who can of Tao the nature tell?
Our sight it flies, our touch as well.
Eluding sight, eluding touch,
The forms of things all in it crouch;
Eluding touch, eluding sight,
There are their semblances, all right.
Profound it is, dark and obscure;
Things' essences all there endure.
Those essences the truth enfold
Of what, when seen, shall then be told.
Now it is so; 'twas so of old.
Its name—what passes not away;
So, in their beautiful array,
Things form and never know decay.

How know I that it is so with all the beauties of existing things? By this (nature of the Tao).

SEAL SCRIPT

47

第二十二章

曲則全，枉則直，窪則盈，敝則新，少則得，多則惑。是以聖人抱一為天下式。不自見，故明；不自是，故彰；不自伐，故有功；不自矜，故長。夫唯不爭，故天下莫能與之爭。古之所謂曲則全者，豈虛言哉!誠全而歸之。

第二十二章

曲则全，枉则直，洼则盈，敝则新，少则得，多则惑。是以圣人抱一为天下式。不自见，故明；不自是，故彰；不自伐，故有功；不自矜，故长。夫唯不争，故天下莫能与之争。古之所谓曲则全者，岂虚言哉!诚全而归之。

XXII

The partial becomes complete; the crooked, straight; the empty, full; the worn out, new. He whose (desires) are few gets them; he whose (desires) are many goes astray.

Therefore the sage holds in his embrace the one thing (of humility), and manifests it to all the world. He is free from self-display, and therefore he shines; from self-assertion, and therefore he is distinguished; from self-boasting, and therefore his merit is acknowledged; from self-complacency, and therefore he acquires superiority. It is because he is thus free from striving that therefore no one in the world is able to strive with him.

That saying of the ancients that 'the partial becomes complete' was not vainly spoken:—all real completion is comprehended under it.

SEAL SCRIPT

第二十三章

希言自然。故飄風不終朝，驟雨不終日。孰為此者?天地。天地尚不能久，而況於人乎?故從事於道者，同於道，德者同於德，失者同於失。同於道者，道亦樂得之;同於德者，德亦樂得之;同於失者，失亦樂得之。信不足焉，有不信焉。

第二十三章

希言自然。故飘风不终朝，骤雨不终日。孰为此者?天地。天地尚不能久，而况于人乎?故从事于道者，同于道，德者同于德，失者同于失。同于道者，道亦乐得之;同于德者，德亦乐得之;同于失者，失亦乐得之。信不足焉，有不信焉。

XXIII

Abstaining from speech marks him who is obeying the spontaneity of his nature. A violent wind does not last for a whole morning; a sudden rain does not last for the whole day. To whom is it that these (two) things are owing? To Heaven and Earth. If Heaven and Earth cannot make such (spasmodic) actings last long, how much less can man!

Therefore when one is making the Tao his business, those who are also pursuing it, agree with him in it, and those who are making the manifestation of its course their object agree with him in that; while even those who are failing in both these things agree with him where they fail.

Hence, those with whom he agrees as to the Tao have the happiness of attaining to it; those with whom he agrees as to its manifestation have the happiness of attaining to it; and those with whom he agrees in their failure have also the happiness of attaining (to the Tao). (But) when there is not faith sufficient (on his part), a want of faith (in him) ensues (on the part of the others).

SEAL SCRIPT

第二十四章

企者不立，跨者不行，自見者不明，自是者不彰，自伐者無功，自矜者不長。其在道也，曰「餘食贅行」。物或惡之，故有道者不處。

第二十四章

企者不立，跨者不行，自见者不明，自是者不彰，自伐者无功，自矜者不长。其在道也，曰「余食赘行」。物或恶之，故有道者不处。

XXIV

He who stands on his tiptoes does not stand firm; he who stretches his legs does not walk (easily). (So), he who displays himself does not shine; he who asserts his own views is not distinguished; he who vaunts himself does not find his merit acknowledged; he who is self-conceited has no superiority allowed to him. Such conditions, viewed from the standpoint of the Tao, are like remnants of food, or a tumour on the body, which all dislike. Hence those who pursue (the course) of the Tao do not adopt and allow them.

SEAL SCRIPT

第二十五章

有物混成，先天地生。寂兮寥兮，獨立而不改，周行而不殆，可以為天下母。吾不知其名，字之曰道，強為之名，曰大。大曰逝，逝曰遠，遠曰反。故道大，天大，地大，王亦大。域中有四大，而王居其一焉。人法地，地法天，天法道，道法自然。

第二十五章

有物混成，先天地生。寂兮寥兮，独立而不改，周行而不殆，可以为天下母。吾不知其名，字之曰道，强为之名，曰大。大曰逝，逝曰远，远曰反。故道大，天大，地大，王亦大。域中有四大，而王居其一焉。人法地，地法天，天法道，道法自然。

XXV

There was something undefined and complete, coming into existence before Heaven and Earth. How still it was and formless, standing alone, and undergoing no change, reaching everywhere and in no danger (of being exhausted)! It may be regarded as the Mother of all things.

I do not know its name, and I give it the designation of the Tao (the Way or Course). Making an effort (further) to give it a name I call it The Great.

Great, it passes on (in constant flow). Passing on, it becomes remote. Having become remote, it returns. Therefore the Tao is great; Heaven is great; Earth is great; and the (sage) king is also great. In the universe there are four that are great, and the (sage) king is one of them.

Man takes his law from the Earth; the Earth takes its law from Heaven; Heaven takes its law from the Tao. The law of the Tao is its being what it is.

SEAL SCRIPT

第二十六章

重為輕根，靜為躁君。是以聖人終日行不離輜重。雖有榮觀，燕處超然。奈何萬乘之主，而以身輕天下?輕則失本，躁則失君。

第二十六章

重为轻根，静为躁君。是以圣人终日行不离辎重。虽有荣观，燕处超然。奈何万乘之主，而以身轻天下?轻则失本，躁则失君。

XXVI

Gravity is the root of lightness; stillness, the ruler of movement.

Therefore a wise prince, marching the whole day, does not go far from his baggage waggons. Although he may have brilliant prospects to look at, he quietly remains (in his proper place), indifferent to them. How should the lord of a myriad chariots carry himself lightly before the kingdom? If he do act lightly, he has lost his root (of gravity); if he proceed to active movement, he will lose his throne.

SEAL SCRIPT

第二十七章

善行無轍跡，善言無瑕讁；善數不用籌策；善閉無關楗而不可開，善結無繩約而不可解。是以聖人常善救人，故無棄人；常善救物，故無棄物，是謂襲明。故善人者，不善人之師；不善人者，善人之資。不貴其師，不愛其資，雖智大迷，是謂要妙。

第二十七章

善行无辙迹，善言无瑕谪；善数不用筹策；善闭无关楗而不可开，善结无绳约而不可解。是以圣人常善救人，故无弃人；常善救物，故无弃物，是谓袭明。故善人者，不善人之师；不善人者，善人之资。不贵其师，不爱其资，虽智大迷，是谓要妙。

XXVII

The skilful traveller leaves no traces of his wheels or footsteps; the skilful speaker says nothing that can be found fault with or blamed; the skilful reckoner uses no tallies; the skilful closer needs no bolts or bars, while to open what he has shut will be impossible; the skilful binder uses no strings or knots, while to unloose what he has bound will be impossible. In the same way the sage is always skilful at saving men, and so he does not cast away any man; he is always skilful at saving things, and so he does not cast away anything. This is called 'Hiding the light of his procedure.'

Therefore the man of skill is a master (to be looked up to) by him who has not the skill; and he who has not the skill is the helper of (the reputation of) him who has the skill. If the one did not honour his master, and the other did not rejoice in his helper, an (observer), though intelligent, might greatly err about them. This is called 'The utmost degree of mystery.'

SEAL SCRIPT

第二十八章

知其雄，守其雌，為天下谿。為天下谿，常德不離，復歸於嬰兒。知其白，守其黑，為天下式。為天下式，常德不忒，復歸於無極。知其榮，守其辱，為天下谷，常德乃足，復歸於樸。樸散則為器，聖人用之，則為官長，故大制不割。

第二十八章

知其雄，守其雌，为天下谿。为天下谿，常德不离，复归于婴儿。知其白，守其黑，为天下式。为天下式，常德不忒，复归于无极。知其荣，守其辱，为天下谷，常德乃足，复归于朴。朴散则为器，圣人用之，则为官长，故大制不割。

XXVIII

Who knows his manhood's strength,
Yet still his female feebleness maintains;
As to one channel flow the many drains,
All come to him, yea, all beneath the sky.
Thus he the constant excellence retains;
The simple child again, free from all stains.

Who knows how white attracts,
Yet always keeps himself within black's shade,
The pattern of humility displayed,
Displayed in view of all beneath the sky;
He in the unchanging excellence arrayed,
Endless return to man's first state has made.

Who knows how glory shines,
Yet loves disgrace, nor e'er for it is pale;
Behold his presence in a spacious vale,
To which men come from all beneath the sky.
The unchanging excellence completes its tale;
The simple infant man in him we hail.

The unwrought material, when divided and distributed, forms vessels. The sage, when employed, becomes the Head of all the Officers (of government); and in his greatest regulations he employs no violent measures.

SEAL SCRIPT

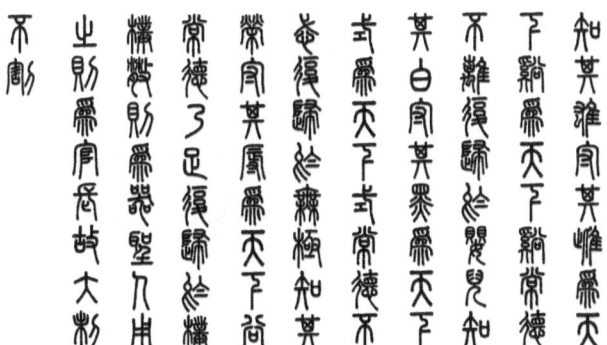

61

第二十九章

　　將欲取天下而為之，吾見其不得已。天下神器，不可為也，不可執也。為者敗之，執者失之。是以聖人無為，故無敗；無執，故無失。故物或行或隨；或歔或吹；或強或羸；或挫或隳。是以聖人去甚，去奢，去泰。

第二十九章

　　将欲取天下而为之，吾见其不得已。天下神器，不可为也，不可执也。为者败之，执者失之。是以圣人无为，故无败；无执，故无失。故物或行或随；或歔或吹；或强或羸；或挫或隳。是以圣人去甚，去奢，去泰。

XXIX

If any one should wish to get the kingdom for himself, and to effect this by what he does, I see that he will not succeed. The kingdom is a spirit-like thing, and cannot be got by active doing. He who would so win it destroys it; he who would hold it in his grasp loses it.

The course and nature of things is such that
What was in front is now behind;
What warmed anon we freezing find.
Strength is of weakness oft the spoil;
The store in ruins mocks our toil.
Hence the sage puts away excessive effort, extravagance, and easy indulgence.

SEAL SCRIPT

第三十章

以道佐人主者，不以兵強天下。其事好遠。師之所處，荊棘生焉。大軍之後，必有凶年。善者果而已，不以取強。果而勿矜，果而勿伐，果而勿驕。果而不得已，果而勿強。物壯則老，是謂不道，不道早已。

第三十章

以道佐人主者，不以兵强天下。其事好远。师之所处，荆棘生焉。大军之后，必有凶年。善者果而已，不以取强。果而勿矜，果而勿伐，果而勿骄。果而不得已，果而勿强。物壮则老，是谓不道，不道早已。

XXX

He who would assist a lord of men in harmony with the Tao will not assert his mastery in the kingdom by force of arms. Such a course is sure to meet with its proper return.

Wherever a host is stationed, briars and thorns spring up. In the sequence of great armies there are sure to be bad years.

A skilful (commander) strikes a decisive blow, and stops. He does not dare (by continuing his operations) to assert and complete his mastery. He will strike the blow, but will be on his guard against being vain or boastful or arrogant in consequence of it. He strikes it as a matter of necessity; he strikes it, but not from a wish for mastery.

When things have attained their strong maturity they become old. This may be said to be not in accordance with the Tao: and what is not in accordance with it soon comes to an end.

SEAL SCRIPT

第三十一章

夫佳兵者，不祥之器，物或惡之，故有道者不處。君子居則貴左，用兵則貴右。兵者不祥之器，非君子之器，不得已而用之，恬淡為上。勝而不美，而美之者，是樂殺人。夫樂殺人者，則不可以得志於天下矣。吉事尚左，凶事尚右。偏將軍居左，上將軍居右，言以喪禮處之。殺人之眾，以哀悲泣之，戰勝，以喪禮處之。

第三十一章

夫佳兵者，不祥之器，物或恶之，故有道者不处。君子居则贵左，用兵则贵右。兵者不祥之器，非君子之器，不得已而用之，恬淡为上。胜而不美，而美之者，是乐杀人。夫乐杀人者，则不可以得志于天下矣。吉事尚左，凶事尚右。偏将军居左，上将军居右，言以丧礼处之。杀人之众，以哀悲泣之，战胜，以丧礼处之。

XXXI

Now arms, however beautiful, are instruments of evil omen, hateful, it may be said, to all creatures. Therefore they who have the Tao do not like to employ them.

The superior man ordinarily considers the left hand the most honourable place, but in time of war the right hand. Those sharp weapons are instruments of evil omen, and not the instruments of the superior man;—he uses them only on the compulsion of necessity. Calm and repose are what he prizes; victory (by force of arms) is to him undesirable. To consider this desirable would be to delight in the slaughter of men; and he who delights in the slaughter of men cannot get his will in the kingdom.

On occasions of festivity to be on the left hand is the prized position; on occasions of mourning, the right hand. The second in command of the army has his place on the left; the general commanding in chief has his on the right;—his place, that is, is assigned to him as in the rites of mourning. He who has killed multitudes of men should weep for them with the bitterest grief; and the victor in battle has his place (rightly) according to those rites.

SEAL SCRIPT

第三十二章

道常無名，樸雖小，天下莫能臣也。侯王若能守之，萬物將自賓。天地相合，以降甘露，民莫之令而自均。始制有名，名亦既有，夫亦將知止，知止所以不殆。譬道之在天下，猶川谷之於江海。

第三十二章

道常无名，朴虽小，天下莫能臣也。侯王若能守之，万物将自宾。天地相合，以降甘露，民莫之令而自均。始制有名，名亦既有，夫亦将知止，知止所以不殆。譬道之在天下，犹川谷之于江海。

XXXII

The Tao, considered as unchanging, has no name.

Though in its primordial simplicity it may be small, the whole world dares not deal with (one embodying) it as a minister. If a feudal prince or the king could guard and hold it, all would spontaneously submit themselves to him.

Heaven and Earth (under its guidance) unite together and send down the sweet dew, which, without the directions of men, reaches equally everywhere as of its own accord.

As soon as it proceeds to action, it has a name. When it once has that name, (men) can know to rest in it. When they know to rest in it, they can be free from all risk of failure and error.

The relation of the Tao to all the world is like that of the great rivers and seas to the streams from the valleys.

SEAL SCRIPT

69

第三十三章

知人者智，自知者明。勝人者有力，自勝者強。知足者富。強行者有志。不失其所者久。死而不亡者壽。

第三十三章

知人者智，自知者明。胜人者有力，自胜者强。知足者富。强行者有志。不失其所者久。死而不亡者寿。

XXXIII

He who knows other men is discerning; he who knows himself is intelligent. He who overcomes others is strong; he who overcomes himself is mighty. He who is satisfied with his lot is rich; he who goes on acting with energy has a (firm) will.

He who does not fail in the requirements of his position, continues long; he who dies and yet does not perish, has longevity.

SEAL SCRIPT

第三十四章

大道氾兮，其可左右。萬物恃之而生而不辭，功成不名有。衣養萬物而不為主，常無欲，可名於小；萬物歸焉而不為主，可名為大。以其終不自為大，故能成其大。

第三十四章

大道泛兮，其可左右。万物恃之而生而不辞，功成不名有。衣养万物而不为主，常无欲，可名于小；万物归焉而不为主，可名为大。以其终不自为大，故能成其大。

XXXIV

All-pervading is the Great Tao! It may be found on the left hand and on the right.

All things depend on it for their production, which it gives to them, not one refusing obedience to it. When its work is accomplished, it does not claim the name of having done it. It clothes all things as with a garment, and makes no assumption of being their lord;—it may be named in the smallest things. All things return (to their root and disappear), and do not know that it is it which presides over their doing so;—it may be named in the greatest things.

Hence the sage is able (in the same way) to accomplish his great achievements. It is through his not making himself great that he can accomplish them.

SEAL SCRIPT

第三十五章

執大象，天下往。往而不害，安平太。樂與餌，過客止。道之出口，淡乎其無味，視之不足見，聽之不足聞，用之不可既。

第三十五章

执大象，天下往。往而不害，安平太。乐与饵，过客止。道之出口，淡乎其无味，视之不足见，听之不足闻，用之不可既。

XXXV

To him who holds in his hands the Great Image (of the invisible Tao), the whole world repairs. Men resort to him, and receive no hurt, but (find) rest, peace, and the feeling of ease.

Music and dainties will make the passing guest stop (for a time). But though the Tao as it comes from the mouth, seems insipid and has no flavour, though it seems not worth being looked at or listened to, the use of it is inexhaustible.

SEAL SCRIPT

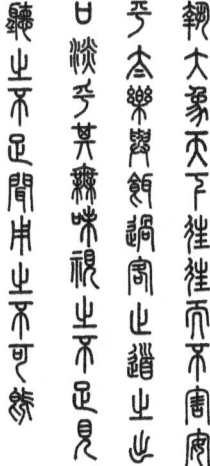

第三十六章

將欲歙之，必固張之；將欲弱之，必固強之；將欲廢之,必固興之;將欲奪之,必固與之。是謂微明。柔弱勝剛強。魚不可脫於淵，國之利器不可以示人。

第三十六章

将欲歙之，必固张之；将欲弱之，必固强之；将欲废之,必固兴之;将欲夺之,必固与之。是谓微明。柔弱胜刚强。鱼不可脱于渊，国之利器不可以示人。

XXXVI

When one is about to take an inspiration, he is sure to make a (previous) expiration; when he is going to weaken another, he will first strengthen him; when he is going to overthrow another, he will first have raised him up; when he is going to despoil another, he will first have made gifts to him:—this is called 'Hiding the light (of his procedure).'

The soft overcomes the hard; and the weak the strong.

Fishes should not be taken from the deep; instruments for the profit of a state should not be shown to the people.

SEAL SCRIPT

第三十七章

道常無為而無不為。侯王若能守之，萬物將自化。化而欲作，吾將鎮之以無名之樸。無名之樸，夫亦將無欲。不欲以靜，天下將自定。

第三十七章

道常无为而无不为。侯王若能守之，万物将自化。化而欲作，吾将镇之以无名之朴。无名之朴，夫亦将无欲。不欲以静，天下将自定。

XXXVII

The Tao in its regular course does nothing (for the sake of doing it), and so there is nothing which it does not do.

If princes and kings were able to maintain it, all things would of themselves be transformed by them.

If this transformation became to me an object of desire, I would express the desire by the nameless simplicity.

Simplicity without a name
Is free from all external aim.
With no desire, at rest and still,
All things go right as of their will.

SEAL SCRIPT

79

第三十八章

上德不德，是以有德；下德不失德，是以無德。上德無為而無以為；下德為之而有以為。上仁為之而無以為；上義為之而有以為。上禮為之而莫之應，則攘臂而扔之。故失道而後德，失德而後仁，失仁而後義，失義而後禮。夫禮者，忠信之薄，而亂之首。前識者，道之華，而愚之始。是以大丈夫處其厚，不居其薄；處其實，不居其華。故去彼取此。

第三十八章

上德不德，是以有德；下德不失德，是以无德。上德无为而无以为；下德为之而有以为。上仁为之而无以为；上义为之而有以为。上礼为之而莫之应，则攘臂而扔之。故失道而后德，失德而后仁，失仁而后义，失义而后礼。夫礼者，忠信之薄，而乱之首。前识者，道之华，而愚之始。是以大丈夫处其厚，不居其薄；处其实，不居其华。故去彼取此。

XXXVIII

(Those who) possessed in highest degree the attributes (of the Tao) did not (seek) to show them, and therefore they possessed them (in fullest measure). (Those who) possessed in a lower degree those attributes (sought how) not to lose them, and therefore they did not possess them (in fullest measure).

(Those who) possessed in the highest degree those attributes did nothing (with a purpose), and had no need to do anything. (Those who) possessed them in a lower degree were (always) doing, and had need to be so doing.

(Those who) possessed the highest benevolence were (always seeking) to carry it out, and had no need to be doing so. (Those who) possessed the highest righteousness were (always seeking) to carry it out, and had need to be so doing.

(Those who) possessed the highest (sense of) propriety were (always seeking) to show it, and when men did not respond to it, they bared the arm and marched up to them.

Thus it was that when the Tao was lost, its attributes appeared; when its attributes were lost, benevolence appeared; when benevolence was lost, righteousness appeared; and when righteousness was lost, the proprieties appeared.

Now propriety is the attenuated form of leal-heartedness and good faith, and is also the commencement of disorder; swift apprehension is (only) a flower of the Tao, and is the beginning of stupidity.

Thus it is that the Great man abides by what is solid, and eschews what is flimsy; dwells with the fruit and not with the flower. It is thus that he puts away the one and makes choice of the other.

SEAL SCRIPT

第三十九章

　　昔之得一者，天得一以清，地得一以寧，神得一以靈，谷得一以盈，萬物得一以生，侯王得一以為天下貞。其致之，天無以清將恐裂，地無以寧將恐發，神無以靈將恐歇，谷無以盈將恐竭，萬物無以生將恐滅，侯王無以貴高將恐蹶。故貴以賤為本，高以下為基。是以侯王自稱孤、　寡、　不穀。此非以賤為本邪？非乎？故致數輿無輿。不欲琭琭如玉，珞珞如石。

第三十九章

　　昔之得一者，天得一以清，地得一以宁，神得一以灵，谷得一以盈，万物得一以生，侯王得一以为天下贞。其致之，天无以清将恐裂，地无以宁将恐发，神无以灵将恐歇，谷无以盈将恐竭，万物无以生将恐灭，侯王无以贵高将恐蹶。故贵以贱为本，高以下为基。是以侯王自称孤、　寡、　不谷。此非以贱为本邪？非乎？故致数舆无舆。不欲琭琭如玉，珞珞如石。

XXXIX

The things which from of old have got the One (the Tao) are—
  Heaven which by it is bright and pure;
  Earth rendered thereby firm and sure;
  Spirits with powers by it supplied;
  Valleys kept full throughout their void
  All creatures which through it do live
  Princes and kings who from it get
  The model which to all they give.
All these are the results of the One (Tao).
  If heaven were not thus pure, it soon would rend;
  If earth were not thus sure, 'twould break and bend;
  Without these powers, the spirits soon would fail;
  If not so filled, the drought would parch each vale;
  Without that life, creatures would pass away;
  Princes and kings, without that moral sway,
  However grand and high, would all decay.

Thus it is that dignity finds its (firm) root in its (previous) meanness, and what is lofty finds its stability in the lowness (from which it rises). Hence princes and kings call themselves 'Orphans,' 'Men of small virtue,' and as 'Carriages without a nave.' Is not this an acknowledgment that in their considering themselves mean they see the foundation of their dignity? So it is that in the enumeration of the different parts of a carriage we do not come on what makes it answer the ends of a carriage. They do not wish to show themselves elegant-looking as jade, but (prefer) to be coarse-looking as an (ordinary) stone.

SEAL SCRIPT

第四十章

反者道之動，弱者道之用。天下萬物生於有，有生於無。

第四十章

反者道之动，弱者道之用。天下万物生于有，有生于无。

XL

The movement of the Tao
    By contraries proceeds;
And weakness marks the course
    Of Tao's mighty deeds.
All things under heaven sprang from It as existing (and named); that existence sprang from It as non-existent (and not named).

SEAL SCRIPT

第四十一章

　　上士聞道，勤而行之；中士聞道，若存若亡；下士聞道，大笑之。不笑，不足以為道。故建言有之:明道若昧，進道若退，夷道若纇，上德若谷，大白若辱，廣德若不足，建德若偷，質真若渝，大方無隅，大器晚成，大音希聲，大象無形，道隱無名。夫唯道，善貸且成。

第四十一章

　　上士闻道，勤而行之；中士闻道，若存若亡；下士闻道，大笑之。不笑，不足以为道。故建言有之:明道若昧，进道若退，夷道若纇，上德若谷，大白若辱，广德若不足，建德若偷，质真若渝，大方无隅，大器晚成，大音希声，大象无形，道隐无名。夫唯道，善贷且成。

XLI

Scholars of the highest class, when they hear about the Tao, earnestly carry it into practice. Scholars of the middle class, when they have heard about it, seem now to keep it and now to lose it. Scholars of the lowest class, when they have heard about it, laugh greatly at it. If it were not (thus) laughed at, it would not be fit to be the Tao.

Therefore the sentence-makers have thus expressed themselves:—

'The Tao, when brightest seen, seems light to lack;
Who progress in it makes, seems drawing back;
Its even way is like a rugged track.
Its highest virtue from the vale doth rise;
Its greatest beauty seems to offend the eyes;
And he has most whose lot the least supplies.
Its firmest virtue seems but poor and low;
Its solid truth seems change to undergo;
Its largest square doth yet no corner show
A vessel great, it is the slowest made;
Loud is its sound, but never word it said;
A semblance great, the shadow of a shade.'

The Tao is hidden, and has no name; but it is the Tao which is skilful at imparting (to all things what they need) and making them complete.

SEAL SCRIPT

87

第四十二章

道生一，一生二，二生三，三生萬物。萬物負陰而抱陽，沖氣以為和。人之所惡，唯孤、寡、不穀，而王公以為稱。故物或損之而益，或益之而損。人之所教，我亦教之。強梁者不得其死，吾將以為教父。

第四十二章

道生一，一生二，二生三，三生万物。万物负阴而抱阳，冲气以为和。人之所恶，唯孤、寡、不谷，而王公以为称。故物或损之而益，或益之而损。人之所教，我亦教之。强梁者不得其死，吾将以为教父。

XLII

The Tao produced One; One produced Two; Two produced Three; Three produced All things. All things leave behind them the Obscurity (out of which they have come), and go forward to embrace the Brightness (into which they have emerged), while they are harmonised by the Breath of Vacancy.

What men dislike is to be orphans, to have little virtue, to be as carriages without naves; and yet these are the designations which kings and princes use for themselves. So it is that some things are increased by being diminished, and others are diminished by being increased.

What other men (thus) teach, I also teaThe violent and strong do not die their natural death. I will make this the basis of my teaching.

SEAL SCRIPT

第四十三章

天下之至柔，馳騁天下之至堅。無有入無閒，吾是以知無為之有益。不言之教，無為之益，天下希及之。

第四十三章

天下之至柔，驰骋天下之至坚。无有入无闲，吾是以知无为之有益。不言之教，无为之益，天下希及之。

XLIII

The softest thing in the world dashes against and overcomes the hardest; that which has no (substantial) existence enters where there is no crevice. I know hereby what advantage belongs to doing nothing (with a purpose).

There are few in the world who attain to the teaching without words, and the advantage arising from non-action.

SEAL SCRIPT

第四十四章

名與身孰親?身與貨孰多?得與亡孰病?是故甚愛必大費,多藏必厚亡,知足不辱,知止不殆,可以長久。

第四十四章

名与身孰亲?身与货孰多?得与亡孰病?是故甚爱必大费,多藏必厚亡,知足不辱,知止不殆,可以长久。

XLIV

Or fame or life,
  Which do you hold more dear?
Or life or wealth,
  To which would you adhere?
Keep life and lose those other things;
Keep them and lose your life:—which brings
  Sorrow and pain more near?

.

Thus we may see,
  Who cleaves to fame
  Rejects what is more great;
Who loves large stores
  Gives up the richer state.

.

Who is content
Needs fear no shame.
Who knows to stop
Incurs no blame.
From danger free
Long live shall he.

SEAL SCRIPT

第四十五章

大成若缺，其用不弊。大盈若沖，其用不窮。大直若屈，大巧若拙，大辯若訥。靜勝躁，寒勝熱。清靜為天下正。

第四十五章

大成若缺，其用不弊。大盈若冲，其用不穷。大直若屈，大巧若拙，大辩若讷。静胜躁，寒胜热。清静为天下正。

XLV

Who thinks his great achievements poor
Shall find his vigour long endure.
Of greatest fulness, deemed a void,
Exhaustion ne'er shall stem the tide.
Do thou what's straight still crooked deem;
Thy greatest art still stupid seem,
And eloquence a stammering scream.
Constant action overcomes cold; being still overcomes heat. Purity and stillness give the correct law to all under heaven.

SEAL SCRIPT

大成若缺其用不弊大盈若
冲其用不窮大直若屈大巧
若拙大辯若訥躁勝寒靜勝
熱清靜為天下正

第四十六章

天下有道，卻走馬以糞。天下無道，戎馬生於郊。禍莫大於不知足；咎莫大於欲得。故知足之足，常足矣。

第四十六章

天下有道，却走马以粪。天下无道，戎马生于郊。祸莫大于不知足；咎莫大于欲得。故知足之足，常足矣。

XLVI

When the Tao prevails in the world, they send back their swift horses to (draw) the dung-carts. When the Tao is disregarded in the world, the war-horses breed in the border lands.

There is no guilt greater than to sanction ambition; no calamity greater than to be discontented with one's lot; no fault greater than the wish to be getting. Therefore the sufficiency of contentment is an enduring and unchanging sufficiency.

SEAL SCRIPT

第四十七章

不出戶，知天下；不窺牖，見天道。其出彌遠，其知彌少。是以聖人不行而知，不見而明，不為而成。

第四十七章

不出户，知天下；不窥牖，见天道。其出弥远，其知弥少。是以圣人不行而知，不见而明，不为而成。

XLVII

Without going outside his door, one understands (all that takes place) under the sky; without looking out from his window, one sees the Tao of Heaven. The farther that one goes out (from himself), the less he knows.

Therefore the sages got their knowledge without travelling; gave their (right) names to things without seeing them; and accomplished their ends without any purpose of doing so.

SEAL SCRIPT

第四十八章

　　為學日益，為道日損。損之又損，以至於無為。無為而無不為。取天下常以無事，及其有事，不足以取天下。

第四十八章

　　为学日益，为道日损。损之又损，以至于无为。无为而无不为。取天下常以无事，及其有事，不足以取天下。

XLVIII

He who devotes himself to learning (seeks) from day to day to increase (his knowledge); he who devotes himself to the Tao (seeks) from day to day to diminish (his doing).

He diminishes it and again diminishes it, till he arrives at doing nothing (on purpose). Having arrived at this point of non-action, there is nothing which he does not do.

He who gets as his own all under heaven does so by giving himself no trouble (with that end). If one take trouble (with that end), he is not equal to getting as his own all under heaven.

SEAL SCRIPT

第四十九章

聖人無常心，以百姓心為心。善者，吾善之；不善者，吾亦善之；德善。信者，吾信之；不信者，吾亦信之；德信。聖人在，天下歙歙焉，為天下渾其心，百姓皆注其耳目，聖人皆孩之。

第四十九章

圣人无常心，以百姓心为心。善者，吾善之；不善者，吾亦善之；德善。信者，吾信之；不信者，吾亦信之；德信。圣人在，天下歙歙焉，为天下浑其心，百姓皆注其耳目，圣人皆孩之。

XLIX

The sage has no invariable mind of his own; he makes the mind of the people his mind.

To those who are good (to me), I am good; and to those who are not good (to me), I am also good;—and thus (all) get to be good. To those who are sincere (with me), I am sincere; and to those who are not sincere (with me), I am also sincere;—and thus (all) get to be sincere.

The sage has in the world an appearance of indecision, and keeps his mind in a state of indifference to all. The people all keep their eyes and ears directed to him, and he deals with them all as his children.

SEAL SCRIPT

第五十章

出生入死。生之徒，十有三；死之徒，十有三；
人之生，動之死地，亦十有三。夫何故?以其生生之
厚。蓋聞善攝生者，陸行不遇兕虎，入軍不被甲兵；
兕無所投其角，虎無所措其爪，兵無所容其刃。夫
何故?以其無死地。

第五十章

出生入死。生之徒，十有三；死之徒，十有三；
人之生，动之死地，亦十有三。夫何故?以其生生之
厚。盖闻善摄生者，陆行不遇兕虎，入军不被甲兵；
兕无所投其角，虎无所措其爪，兵无所容其刃。夫
何故?以其无死地。

L

Men come forth and live; they enter (again) and die.

Of every ten three are ministers of life (to themselves); and three are ministers of death.

There are also three in every ten whose aim is to live, but whose movements tend to the land (or place) of death. And for what reason? Because of their excessive endeavours to perpetuate life.

But I have heard that he who is skilful in managing the life entrusted to him for a time travels on the land without having to shun rhinoceros or tiger, and enters a host without having to avoid buff coat or sharp weapon. The rhinoceros finds no place in him into which to thrust its horn, nor the tiger a place in which to fix its claws, nor the weapon a place to admit its point. And for what reason? Because there is in him no place of death.

SEAL SCRIPT

第五十一章

　　道生之，德畜之，物形之，勢成之。是以萬物莫不尊道而貴德。道之尊，德之貴，夫莫之命而常自然。故道生之，德畜之。長之育之，亭之毒之，養之覆之。生而不有，為而不恃，長而不宰。是謂玄德。

第五十一章

　　道生之，德畜之，物形之，势成之。是以万物莫不尊道而贵德。道之尊，德之贵，夫莫之命而常自然。故道生之，德畜之。长之育之，亭之毒之，养之覆之。生而不有，为而不恃，长而不宰。是谓玄德。

LI

All things are produced by the Tao, and nourished by its outflowing operation. They receive their forms according to the nature of each, and are completed
according to the circumstances of their condition. Therefore all things without
exception honour the Tao, and exalt its outflowing operation.

This honouring of the Tao and exalting of its operation is not the result of
any ordination, but always a spontaneous tribute.

Thus it is that the Tao produces (all things), nourishes them, brings them to
their full growth, nurses them, completes them, matures them, maintains them,
and overspreads them.

It produces them and makes no claim to the possession of them; it carries
them through their processes and does not vaunt its ability in doing so; it brings
them to maturity and exercises no control over them;—this is called its mysterious operation.

SEAL SCRIPT

第五十二章

天下有始，以為天下母。既得其母，以知其子，既知其子，復守其母，沒身不殆。塞其兌，閉其門，終身不勤。開其兌，濟其事，終身不救。見小曰明，守柔曰強。用其光，復歸其明，無遺身殃，是為習常。

第五十二章

天下有始，以为天下母。既得其母，以知其子，既知其子，复守其母，没身不殆。塞其兑，闭其门，终身不勤。开其兑，济其事，终身不救。见小曰明，守柔曰强。用其光，复归其明，无遗身殃，是为习常。

LII

(The Tao) which originated all under the sky is to be considered as the mother of them all.

When the mother is found, we know what her children should be. When one knows that he is his mother's child, and proceeds to guard (the qualities of) the mother that belong to him, to the end of his life he will be free from all peril.

Let him keep his mouth closed, and shut up the portals (of his nostrils), and all his life he will be exempt from laborious exertion. Let him keep his mouth open, and (spend his breath) in the promotion of his affairs, and all his life there will be no safety for him.

The perception of what is small is (the secret of) clear-sightedness; the guarding of what is soft and tender is (the secret of) strength.

Who uses well his light,
Reverting to its (source so) bright,
Will from his body ward all blight,
And hides the unchanging from men's sight.

SEAL SCRIPT

109

第五十三章

使我介然有知，行於大道，唯施是畏。大道甚夷，
而人好徑。朝甚除，田甚蕪，倉甚虛；服文綵，帶利劍，
厭飲食，財貨有餘；是為夸盜。非道也哉！

第五十三章

使我介然有知，行于大道，唯施是畏。大道甚夷，
而人好径。朝甚除，田甚芜，仓甚虚；服文彩，带利剑，
厌饮食，财货有余；是为夸盗。非道也哉！

LIII

If I were suddenly to become known, and (put into a position to) conduct (a government) according to the Great Tao, what I should be most afraid of would be a boastful display.

The great Tao (or way) is very level and easy; but people love the by-ways.

Their court(-yards and buildings) shall be well kept, but their fields shall be ill-cultivated, and their granaries very empty. They shall wear elegant and ornamented robes, carry a sharp sword at their girdle, pamper themselves in eating and drinking, and have a superabundance of property and wealth;—such (princes) may be called robbers and boasters. This is contrary to the Tao surely!

SEAL SCRIPT

第五十四章

　　善建者不拔，善抱者不脱，子孫以祭祀不輟。修之於身，其德乃真；修之於家，其德乃餘；修之於鄉，其德乃長；修之於國，其德乃豐；修之於天下，其德乃普。故以身觀身，以家觀家，以鄉觀鄉，以國觀國，以天下觀天下。吾何以知天下然哉?以此。

第五十四章

　　善建者不拔，善抱者不脱，子孙以祭祀不辍。修之于身，其德乃真；修之于家，其德乃余；修之于乡，其德乃长；修之于国，其德乃丰；修之于天下，其德乃普。故以身观身，以家观家，以乡观乡，以国观国，以天下观天下。吾何以知天下然哉?以此。

LIV

What (Tao's) skilful planter plants
  Can never be uptorn;
What his skilful arms enfold,
  From him can ne'er be borne.
Sons shall bring in lengthening line,
Sacrifices to his shrine.

.

Tao when nursed within one's self,
  His vigour will make true;
And where the family it rules
  What riches will accrue!
The neighbourhood where it prevails
  In thriving will abound;
And when 'tis seen throughout the state,
  Good fortune will be found.
Employ it the kingdom o'er,
  And men thrive all around.

In this way the effect will be seen in the person, by the observation of different cases; in the family; in the neighbourhood; in the state; and in the kingdom.

How do I know that this effect is sure to hold thus all under the sky? By this (method of observation).

SEAL SCRIPT

113

第五十五章

　　含德之厚，比於赤子。蜂蠆虺蛇不螫，猛獸不據，攫鳥不搏。骨弱筋柔而握固。未知牝牡之合而全作，精之至也。終日號而不嗄，和之至也。知和曰常，知常曰明。益生曰祥。心使氣曰強。物壯則老，謂之不道，不道早已。

第五十五章

　　含德之厚，比于赤子。蜂虿虺蛇不螫，猛兽不据，攫鸟不搏。骨弱筋柔而握固。未知牝牡之合而全作，精之至也。终日号而不嗄，和之至也。知和曰常，知常曰明。益生曰祥。心使气曰强。物壮则老，谓之不道，不道早已。

LV

He who has in himself abundantly the attributes (of the Tao) is like an infant. Poisonous insects will not sting him; fierce beasts will not seize him; birds of prey will not strike him.

(The infant's) bones are weak and its sinews soft, but yet its grasp is firm. It knows not yet the union of male and female, and yet its virile member may be excited;—showing the perfection of its physical essence. All day long it will cry without its throat becoming hoarse;—showing the harmony (in its constitution).

> To him by whom this harmony is known,
> (The secret of) the unchanging (Tao) is shown,
> And in the knowledge wisdom finds its throne.
> All life-increasing arts to evil turn;
> Where the mind makes the vital breath to burn,
> (False) is the strength, (and o'er it we should mourn.)

When things have become strong, they (then) become old, which may be said to be contrary to the Tao. Whatever is contrary to the Tao soon ends.

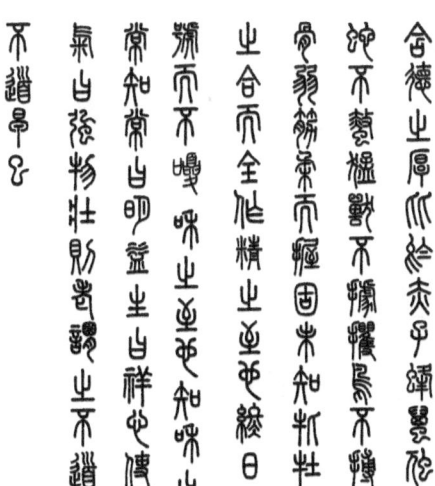

第五十六章

知者不言，言者不知。塞其兑，閉其門，挫其銳，解其分，和其光，同其塵，是謂玄同。故不可得而親，不可得而疏；不可得而利，不可得而害；不可得而貴，不可得而賤。故為天下貴。

第五十六章

知者不言，言者不知。塞其兑，闭其门，挫其锐，解其分，和其光，同其尘，是谓玄同。故不可得而亲，不可得而疏；不可得而利，不可得而害；不可得而贵，不可得而贱。故为天下贵。

LVI

He who knows (the Tao) does not (care to) speak (about it); he who is (ever ready to) speak about it does not know it.

He (who knows it) will keep his mouth shut and close the portals (of his nostrils). He will blunt his sharp points and unravel the complications of things; he will attemper his brightness, and bring himself into agreement with the obscurity (of others). This is called 'the Mysterious Agreement.'

(Such an one) cannot be treated familiarly or distantly; he is beyond all consideration of profit or injury; of nobility or meanness:—he is the noblest man under heaven.

SEAL SCRIPT

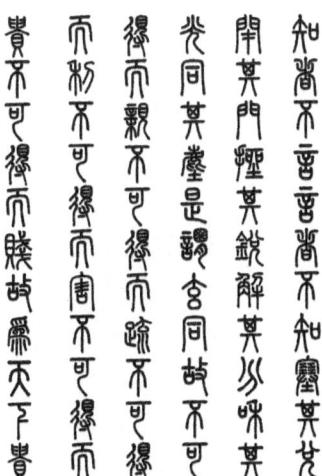

第五十七章

以正治國，以奇用兵，以無事取天下。吾何以知其然哉?以此。天下多忌諱，而民彌貧；民多利器，國家滋昏；人多伎巧,奇物滋起;法令滋彰,盜賊多有。故聖人云:「我無為，而民自化；我好靜，而民自正；我無事，而民自富；我無欲，而民自樸。」

第五十七章

以正治国，以奇用兵，以无事取天下。吾何以知其然哉?以此。天下多忌讳，而民弥贫；民多利器，国家滋昏；人多伎巧,奇物滋起;法令滋彰,盗贼多有。故圣人云:「我无为，而民自化；我好静，而民自正；我无事，而民自富；我无欲，而民自朴。」

LVII

A state may be ruled by (measures of) correction; weapons of war may be used with crafty dexterity; (but) the kingdom is made one's own (only) by freedom from action and purpose.

How do I know that it is so? By these facts:—In the kingdom the multiplication of prohibitive enactments increases the poverty of the people; the more implements to add to their profit that the people have, the greater disorder is there in the state and clan; the more acts of crafty dexterity that men possess, the more do strange contrivances appear; the more display there is of legislation, the more thieves and robbers there are.

Therefore a sage has said, 'I will do nothing (of purpose), and the people will be transformed of themselves; I will be fond of keeping still, and the people will of themselves become correct. I will take no trouble about it, and the people will of themselves become rich; I will manifest no ambition, and the people will of themselves attain to the primitive simplicity.'

SEAL SCRIPT

第五十八章

其政悶悶，其民淳淳；其政察察，其民缺缺。
禍兮福之所倚，福兮禍之所伏。孰知其極?其無正。
正復為奇，善復為妖。人之迷，其日固久。是以聖
人方而不割，廉而不劌，直而不肆，光而不燿。

第五十八章

其政闷闷，其民淳淳；其政察察，其民缺缺。
祸兮福之所倚，福兮祸之所伏。孰知其极?其无正。
正复为奇，善复为妖。人之迷，其日固久。是以圣
人方而不割，廉而不刿，直而不肆，光而不燿。

LVIII

The government that seems the most unwise,
Oft goodness to the people best supplies;
That which is meddling, touching everything,
Will work but ill, and disappointment bring.

Misery!—happiness is to be found by its side! Happiness!—misery lurks beneath it! Who knows what either will come to in the end?

Shall we then dispense with correction? The (method of) correction shall by a turn become distortion, and the good in it shall by a turn become evil. The delusion of the people (on this point) has indeed subsisted for a long time.

Therefore the sage is (like) a square which cuts no one (with its angles); (like) a corner which injures no one (with its sharpness). He is straightforward, but allows himself no license; he is bright, but does not dazzle.

SEAL SCRIPT

第五十九章

治人事天，莫若嗇。夫唯嗇，是謂早服；早服謂之重積德；重積德則無不克；無不克則莫知其極；莫知其極，可以有國；有國之母，可以長久；是謂深根固柢，長生久視之道。

第五十九章

治人事天，莫若啬。夫唯啬，是谓早服；早服谓之重积德；重积德则无不克；无不克则莫知其极；莫知其极，可以有国；有国之母，可以长久；是谓深根固柢，长生久视之道。

LIX

For regulating the human (in our constitution) and rendering the (proper) service to the heavenly, there is nothing like moderation.

It is only by this moderation that there is effected an early return (to man's normal state). That early return is what I call the repeated accumulation of the attributes (of the Tao). With that repeated accumulation of those attributes, there comes the subjugation (of every obstacle to such return). Of this subjugation we know not what shall be the limit; and when one knows not what the limit shall be, he may be the ruler of a state.

He who possesses the mother of the state may continue long. His case is like that (of the plant) of which we say that its roots are deep and its flower stalks firm:—this is the way to secure that its enduring life shall long be seen.

SEAL SCRIPT

第六十章

治大國，若烹小鮮。以道蒞天下，其鬼不神；非其鬼不神，其神不傷人；非其神不傷人，聖人亦不傷人。夫兩不相傷，故德交歸焉。

第六十章

治大国，若烹小鲜。以道莅天下，其鬼不神；非其鬼不神，其神不伤人；非其神不伤人，圣人亦不伤人。夫两不相伤，故德交归焉。

LX

Governing a great state is like cooking small fish.

Let the kingdom be governed according to the Tao, and the manes of the departed will not manifest their spiritual energy. It is not that those manes have not that spiritual energy, but it will not be employed to hurt men. It is not that it could not hurt men, but neither does the ruling sage hurt them.

When these two do not injuriously affect each other, their good influences converge in the virtue (of the Tao).

SEAL SCRIPT

第六十一章

　　大國者下流，天下之交。天下之牝，牝常以靜勝牡，以靜為下。故大國以下小國，則取小國；小國以下大國，則取大國。故或下以取，或下而取。大國不過欲兼畜人，小國不過欲入事人。夫兩者各得其所欲，大者宜為下。

第六十一章

　　大国者下流，天下之交。天下之牝，牝常以静胜牡，以静为下。故大国以下小国，则取小国；小国以下大国，则取大国。故或下以取，或下而取。大国不过欲兼畜人，小国不过欲入事人。夫两者各得其所欲，大者宜为下。

LXI

What makes a great state is its being (like) a low-lying, down-flowing (stream);—it becomes the centre to which tend (all the small states) under heaven.

(To illustrate from) the case of all females:—the female always overcomes the male by her stillness. Stillness may be considered (a sort of) abasement.

Thus it is that a great state, by condescending to small states, gains them for itself; and that small states, by abasing themselves to a great state, win it over to them. In the one case the abasement leads to gaining adherents, in the other case to procuring favour.

The great state only wishes to unite men together and nourish them; a small state only wishes to be received by, and to serve, the other. Each gets what it desires, but the great state must learn to abase itself.

SEAL SCRIPT

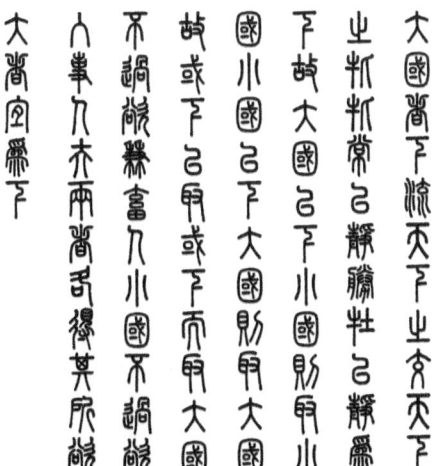

第六十二章

道者萬物之奧。善人之寶，不善人之所保。美言可以市，尊行可以加人。人之不善，何棄之有?故立天子,置三公,雖有拱璧以先駟馬,不如坐進此道。古之所以貴此道者何?不曰:以求得，有罪以免邪?故為天下貴。

第六十二章

道者万物之奥。善人之宝，不善人之所保。美言可以市，尊行可以加人。人之不善，何弃之有?故立天子,置三公,虽有拱璧以先驷马,不如坐进此道。古之所以贵此道者何?不曰:以求得，有罪以免邪?故为天下贵。

LXII

Tao has of all things the most honoured place.
No treasures give good men so rich a grace;
Bad men it guards, and doth their ill efface.

(Its) admirable words can purchase honour; (its) admirable deeds can raise their performer above others. Even men who are not good are not abandoned by it.

Therefore when the sovereign occupies his place as the Son of Heaven, and he has appointed his three ducal ministers, though (a prince) were to send in a round symbol-of-rank large enough to fill both the hands, and that as the precursor of the team of horses (in the court-yard), such an offering would not be equal to (a lesson of) this Tao, which one might present on his knees.

Why was it that the ancients prized this Tao so much? Was it not because it could be got by seeking for it, and the guilty could escape (from the stain of their guilt) by it? This is the reason why all under heaven consider it the most valuable thing.

SEAL SCRIPT

129

第六十三章

為無為，事無事，味無味。大小多少，報怨以德。圖難於其易，為大於其細；天下難事必作於易，天下大事必作於細。是以聖人終不為大，故能成其大。夫輕諾必寡信，多易必多難。是以聖人猶難之，故終無難矣。

第六十三章

为无为，事无事，味无味。大小多少，报怨以德。图难于其易，为大于其细；天下难事必作于易，天下大事必作于细。是以圣人终不为大，故能成其大。夫轻诺必寡信，多易必多难。是以圣人犹难之，故终无难矣。

LXIII

(It is the way of the Tao) to act without (thinking of) acting; to conduct affairs without (feeling the) trouble of them; to taste without discerning any flavour; to consider what is small as great, and a few as many; and to recompense injury with kindness.

(The master of it) anticipates things that are difficult while they are easy, and does things that would become great while they are small. All difficult things in the world are sure to arise from a previous state in which they were easy, and all great things from one in which they were small. Therefore the sage, while he never does what is great, is able on that account to accomplish the greatest things.

He who lightly promises is sure to keep but little faith; he who is continually thinking things easy is sure to find them difficult. Therefore the sage sees difficulty even in what seems easy, and so never has any difficulties.

SEAL SCRIPT

難其
輕
是
己
聖
人
猶
難
止
故
終
無
難

大
木
輕
諾
必
寡
信
多
易
必
多

己
聖
人
終
不
為
大
故
能
成
其

終
易
天
下
大
事
必
作
於
是

需
大
於
其
細
天
下
難
事
必
作
於

多
少
報
怨
己
德
圖
難
於
其
易

需
需
需
事
無
事
需
需
需
無
大
小

第六十四章

其安易持，其未兆易謀。其脆易泮，其微易散。
為之於未有，治之於未亂。合抱之木，生於毫末；
九層之臺，起於累土；千里之行，始於足下。為者
敗之，執者失之。是以聖人無為故無敗，無執故無失。
民之從事，常於幾成而敗之。慎終如始，則無敗事。
是以聖人欲不欲，不貴難得之貨；學不學，復眾人
之所過。以輔萬物之自然，而不敢為。

第六十四章

其安易持，其未兆易谋。其脆易泮，其微易散。
为之于未有，治之于未乱。合抱之木，生于毫末；
九层之台，起于累土；千里之行，始于足下。为者
败之，执者失之。是以圣人无为故无败，无执故无失。
民之从事，常于几成而败之。慎终如始，则无败事。
是以圣人欲不欲，不贵难得之货；学不学，复众人
之所过。以辅万物之自然，而不敢为。

LXIV

That which is at rest is easily kept hold of; before a thing has given indications of its presence, it is easy to take measures against it; that which is brittle is easily broken; that which is very small is easily dispersed. Action should be taken before a thing has made its appearance; order should be secured before disorder has begun.

The tree which fills the arms grew from the tiniest sprout; the tower of nine storeys rose from a (small) heap of earth; the journey of a thousand li commenced with a single step.

He who acts (with an ulterior purpose) does harm; he who takes hold of a thing (in the same way) loses his hold. The sage does not act (so), and therefore does no harm; he does not lay hold (so), and therefore does not lose his hold. (But) people in their conduct of affairs are constantly ruining them when they are on the eve of success. If they were careful at the end, as (they should be) at the beginning, they would not so ruin them.

Therefore the sage desires what (other men) do not desire, and does not prize things difficult to get; he learns what (other men) do not learn, and turns back to what the multitude of men have passed by. Thus he helps the natural development of all things, and does not dare to act (with an ulterior purpose of his own).

SEAL SCRIPT

第六十五章

古之善為道者，非以明民，將以愚之。民之難治，以其智多。故以智治國，國之賊；不以智治國，國之福。知此兩者亦稽式。常知稽式，是謂玄德。玄德深矣，遠矣，與物反矣，然後乃至大順。

第六十五章

古之善为道者，非以明民，将以愚之。民之难治，以其智多。故以智治国，国之贼；不以智治国，国之福。知此两者亦稽式。常知稽式，是谓玄德。玄德深矣，远矣，与物反矣，然后乃至大顺。

LXV

The ancients who showed their skill in practising the Tao did so, not to en-
lighten the people, but rather to make them simple and ignorant.

The difficulty in governing the people arises from their having much knowledge. He who (tries to) govern a state by his wisdom is a scourge to it; while he
who does not (try to) do so is a blessing.

He who knows these two things finds in them also his model and rule. Ability to know this model and rule constitutes what we call the mysterious excellence
(of a governor). Deep and far-reaching is such mysterious excellence, showing
indeed its possessor as opposite to others, but leading them to a great conformity
to him.

SEAL SCRIPT

第六十六章

江海所以能為百谷王者，以其善下之，故能為百谷王。是以欲上民，必以言下之。欲先民，必以身後之。是以聖人處上而民不重，處前而民不害。是以天下樂推而不厭，以其不爭，故天下莫能與之爭。

第六十六章

江海所以能为百谷王者，以其善下之，故能为百谷王。是以欲上民，必以言下之。欲先民，必以身后之。是以圣人处上而民不重，处前而民不害。是以天下乐推而不厌，以其不争，故天下莫能与之争。

LXVI

That whereby the rivers and seas are able to receive the homage and tribute of all the valley streams, is their skill in being lower than they;—it is thus that they are the kings of them all. So it is that the sage (ruler), wishing to be above men, puts himself by his words below them, and, wishing to be before them, places his person behind them.

In this way though he has his place above them, men do not feel his weight, nor though he has his place before them, do they feel it an injury to them.

Therefore all in the world delight to exalt him and do not weary of him. Because he does not strive, no one finds it possible to strive with him.

SEAL SCRIPT

第六十七章

天下皆謂我道大，似不肖。夫唯大，故似不肖。若肖，久矣其細也夫！我有三寶，持而保之。一曰慈，二曰儉，三曰不敢為天下先。慈故能勇；儉故能廣；不敢為天下先，故能成器長。今舍慈且勇，舍儉且廣，舍後且先，死矣！夫慈以戰則勝，以守則固。天將救之，以慈衛之。

第六十七章

天下皆谓我道大，似不肖。夫唯大，故似不肖。若肖，久矣其细也夫！我有三宝，持而保之。一曰慈，二曰俭，三曰不敢为天下先。慈故能勇；俭故能广；不敢为天下先，故能成器长。今舍慈且勇，舍俭且广，舍后且先，死矣！夫慈以战则胜，以守则固。天将救之，以慈卫之。

LXVII

All the world says that, while my Tao is great, it yet appears to be inferior (to other systems of teaching). Now it is just its greatness that makes it seem to be inferior. If it were like any other (system), for long would its smallness have been known!

But I have three precious things which I prize and hold fast. The first is gentleness; the second is economy; and the third is shrinking from taking precedence of others.

With that gentleness I can be bold; with that economy I can be liberal; shrinking from taking precedence of others, I can become a vessel of the highest honour. Now-a-days they give up gentleness and are all for being bold; economy, and are all for being liberal; the hindmost place, and seek only to be foremost;—(of all which the end is) death.

Gentleness is sure to be victorious even in battle, and firmly to maintain its ground. Heaven will save its possessor, by his (very) gentleness protecting him.

SEAL SCRIPT

139

第六十八章

善為士者不武，善戰者不怒，善勝敵者不與，善用人者為之下，是謂不爭之德，是謂用人之力，是謂配天古之極。

第六十八章

善为士者不武，善战者不怒，善胜敌者不与，善用人者为之下，是谓不争之德，是谓用人之力，是谓配天古之极。

LXVIII

He who in (Tao's) wars has skill
  Assumes no martial port;
He who fights with most good will
  To rage makes no resort.
He who vanquishes yet still
  Keeps from his foes apart;
He whose hests men most fulfil
  Yet humbly plies his art.

Thus we say, 'He ne'er contends,
  And therein is his might.'
Thus we say, 'Men's wills he bends,
  That they with him unite.'
Thus we say, 'Like Heaven's his ends,
  No sage of old more bright.'

SEAL SCRIPT

第六十九章

　　用兵有言：「吾不敢為主而為客，不敢進寸而退尺。」是謂行無行，攘無臂，扔無敵，執無兵。禍莫大於輕敵，輕敵幾喪吾寶。故抗兵相加，哀者勝矣。

第六十九章

　　用兵有言：「吾不敢为主而为客，不敢进寸而退尺。」是谓行无行，攘无臂，扔无敌，执无兵。祸莫大于轻敌，轻敌几丧吾宝。故抗兵相加，哀者胜矣。

LXIX

A master of the art of war has said, 'I do not dare to be the host (to commence the war); I prefer to be the guest (to act on the defensive). I do not dare to advance an inch; I prefer to retire a foot.' This is called marshalling the ranks where there are no ranks; baring the arms (to fight) where there are no arms to bare; grasping the weapon where there is no weapon to grasp; advancing against the enemy where there is no enemy.

There is no calamity greater than lightly engaging in war. To do that is near losing (the gentleness) which is so precious. Thus it is that when opposing weapons are (actually) crossed, he who deplores (the situation) conquers.

第七十章

　　吾言甚易知，甚易行。天下莫能知，莫能行。言有宗，事有君。夫唯無知，是以不我知。知我者希，則我者貴。是以聖人被褐懷玉。

第七十章

　　吾言甚易知，甚易行。天下莫能知，莫能行。言有宗，事有君。夫唯无知，是以不我知。知我者希，则我者贵。是以圣人被褐怀玉。

LXX

My words are very easy to know, and very easy to practise; but there is no one in the world who is able to know and able to practise them.

There is an originating and all-comprehending (principle) in my words, and an authoritative law for the things (which I enforce). It is because they do not know these, that men do not know me.

They who know me are few, and I am on that account (the more) to be prized. It is thus that the sage wears (a poor garb of) hair cloth, while he carries his (signet of) jade in his bosom.

SEAL SCRIPT

第七十一章

知不知上，不知知病。夫唯病病，是以不病。
聖人不病，以其病病，是以不病。

第七十一章

知不知上，不知知病。夫唯病病，是以不病。
圣人不病，以其病病，是以不病。

LXXI

To know and yet (think) we do not know is the highest (attainment); not to know (and yet think) we do know is a disease.

It is simply by being pained at (the thought of) having this disease that we are preserved from it. The sage has not the disease. He knows the pain that would be inseparable from it, and therefore he does not have it.

SEAL SCRIPT

病病是己不病

病是己不病聖人不病己其

知不知上不知知病夫唯病

第七十二章

民不畏威，則大威至。無狎其所居，無厭其所生。夫唯不厭，是以不厭。是以聖人自知不自見；自愛不自貴。故去彼取此。

第七十二章

民不畏威，则大威至。无狎其所居，无厌其所生。夫唯不厌，是以不厌。是以圣人自知不自见；自爱不自贵。故去彼取此。

LXXII

When the people do not fear what they ought to fear, that which is their great dread will come on them.

Let them not thoughtlessly indulge themselves in their ordinary life; let them not act as if weary of what that life depends on.

It is by avoiding such indulgence that such weariness does not arise.

Therefore the sage knows (these things) of himself, but does not parade (his knowledge); loves, but does not (appear to set a) value on, himself. And thus he puts the latter alternative away and makes choice of the former.

SEAL SCRIPT

149

第七十三章

勇於敢則殺，勇於不敢則活。此兩者，或利或害。天之所惡，孰知其故？是以聖人猶難之。天之道，不爭而善勝，不言而善應，不召而自來，繟然而善謀。天網恢恢，疏而不失。

第七十三章

勇于敢则杀，勇于不敢则活。此两者，或利或害。天之所恶，孰知其故？是以圣人犹难之。天之道，不争而善胜，不言而善应，不召而自来，繟然而善谋。天网恢恢，疏而不失。

LXXIII

He whose boldness appears in his daring (to do wrong, in defiance of the laws) is put to death; he whose boldness appears in his not daring (to do so) lives on. Of these two cases the one appears to be advantageous, and the other to be injurious. But

When Heaven's anger smites a man,

Who the cause shall truly scan?

On this account the sage feels a difficulty (as to what to do in the former case).

It is the way of Heaven not to strive, and yet it skilfully overcomes; not to speak, and yet it is skilful in obtaining a reply; does not call, and yet men come to it of themselves. Its demonstrations are quiet, and yet its plans are skilful and effective. The meshes of the net of Heaven are large; far apart, but letting nothing escape.

SEAL SCRIPT

第七十四章

民不畏死，奈何以死懼之？若使民常畏死，而為奇者，吾得執而殺之，孰敢？常有司殺者殺。夫代司殺者殺，是謂代大匠斲，夫代大匠斲者，希有不傷其手矣。

第七十四章

民不畏死，奈何以死惧之？若使民常畏死，而为奇者，吾得执而杀之，孰敢？常有司杀者杀。夫代司杀者杀，是谓代大匠斲，夫代大匠斲者，希有不伤其手矣。

LXXIV

The people do not fear death; to what purpose is it to (try to) frighten them with death? If the people were always in awe of death, and I could always seize those who do wrong, and put them to death, who would dare to do wrong?

There is always One who presides over the infliction of death. He who would inflict death in the room of him who so presides over it may be described as hewing wood instead of a great carpenter. Seldom is it that he who undertakes the hewing, instead of the great carpenter, does not cut his own hands!

SEAL SCRIPT

第七十五章

民之饑，以其上食稅之多，是以饑。民之難治，以其上之有為，是以難治。民之輕死，以其求生之厚，是以輕死。夫唯無以生為者，是賢於貴生。

第七十五章

民之饥，以其上食税之多，是以饥。民之难治，以其上之有为，是以难治。民之轻死，以其求生之厚，是以轻死。夫唯无以生为者，是贤于贵生。

LXXV

The people suffer from famine because of the multitude of taxes consumed by their superiors. It is through this that they suffer famine.

The people are difficult to govern because of the (excessive) agency of their superiors (in governing them). It is through this that they are difficult to govern.

The people make light of dying because of the greatness of their labours in seeking for the means of living. It is this which makes them think light of dying. Thus it is that to leave the subject of living altogether out of view is better than to set a high value on it.

SEAL SCRIPT

第七十六章

人之生也柔弱，其死也堅強。萬物草木之生也柔脆，其死也枯槁。故堅強者死之徒，柔弱者生之徒。是以兵強則不勝，木強則兵。強大處下，柔弱處上。

第七十六章

人之生也柔弱，其死也坚强。万物草木之生也柔脆，其死也枯槁。故坚强者死之徒，柔弱者生之徒。是以兵强则不胜，木强则兵。强大处下，柔弱处上。

LXXVI

Man at his birth is supple and weak; at his death, firm and strong. (So it is with) all things. Trees and plants, in their early growth, are soft and brittle; at their death, dry and withered.

Thus it is that firmness and strength are the concomitants of death; softness and weakness, the concomitants of life.

Hence he who (relies on) the strength of his forces does not conquer; and a tree which is strong will fill the out-stretched arms, (and thereby invites the feller.)

Therefore the place of what is firm and strong is below, and that of what is soft and weak is above.

SEAL SCRIPT

第七十七章

天之道，其猶張弓與?高者抑之，下者舉之；有餘者損之，不足者補之。天之道，損有餘而補不足。人之道則不然，損不足以奉有餘。孰能有餘以奉天下，唯有道者。是以聖人為而不恃，功成而不處，其不欲見賢。

第七十七章

天之道，其犹张弓与?高者抑之，下者举之；有余者损之，不足者补之。天之道，损有余而补不足。人之道则不然，损不足以奉有余。孰能有余以奉天下，唯有道者。是以圣人为而不恃，功成而不处，其不欲见贤。

LXXVII

May not the Way (or Tao) of Heaven be compared to the (method of) bending a bow? The (part of the bow) which was high is brought low, and what was low is raised up. (So Heaven) diminishes where there is superabundance, and supplements where there is deficiency.

It is the Way of Heaven to diminish superabundance, and to supplement deficiency. It is not so with the way of man. He takes away from those who have not enough to add to his own superabundance.

Who can take his own superabundance and therewith serve all under heaven? Only he who is in possession of the Tao!

Therefore the (ruling) sage acts without claiming the results as his; he achieves his merit and does not rest (arrogantly) in it:—he does not wish to display his superiority.

SEAL SCRIPT

第七十八章

天下莫柔弱於水，而攻堅強者莫之能勝，以其無以易之。弱之勝強，柔之勝剛，天下莫不知莫能行。是以聖人云：「受國之垢，是謂社稷主；受國不祥，是為天下王。」正言若反。

第七十八章

天下莫柔弱于水，而攻坚强者莫之能胜，以其无以易之。弱之胜强，柔之胜刚，天下莫不知莫能行。是以圣人云：「受国之垢，是谓社稷主；受国不祥，是为天下王。」正言若反。

LXXVIII

There is nothing in the world more soft and weak than water, and yet for attacking things that are firm and strong there is nothing that can take precedence of it;—for there is nothing (so effectual) for which it can be changed.

Every one in the world knows that the soft overcomes the hard, and the weak the strong, but no one is able to carry it out in practice.

Therefore a sage has said,
'He who accepts his state's reproach,
 Is hailed therefore its altars' lord;
To him who bears men's direful woes
 They all the name of King accord.'
Words that are strictly true seem to be paradoxical.

SEAL SCRIPT

第七十九章

　　和大怨，必有餘怨，安可以為善?是以聖人執左契，而不責於人。有德司契，無德司徹。天道無親，常與善人。

第七十九章

　　和大怨，必有余怨，安可以为善?是以圣人执左契，而不责于人。有德司契，无德司彻。天道无亲，常与善人。

LXXIX

When a reconciliation is effected (between two parties) after a great animosity, there is sure to be a grudge remaining (in the mind of the one who was wrong). And how can this be beneficial (to the other)?

Therefore (to guard against this), the sage keeps the left-hand portion of the record of the engagement, and does not insist on the (speedy) fulfilment of it by the other party. (So), he who has the attributes (of the Tao) regards (only) the conditions of the engagement, while he who has not those attributes regards only the conditions favourable to himself.

In the Way of Heaven, there is no partiality of love; it is always on the side of the good man.

SEAL SCRIPT

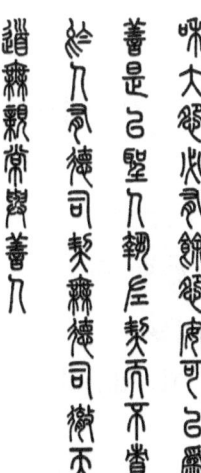

第八十章

　　小國寡民。使有什伯之器而不用，使民重死而不遠徙。雖有舟輿，無所乘之，雖有甲兵，無所陳之。使人復結繩而用之，甘其食，美其服，安其居，樂其俗。鄰國相望，雞犬之聲相聞，民至老死，不相往來。

第八十章

　　小国寡民。使有什伯之器而不用，使民重死而不远徙。虽有舟舆，无所乘之，虽有甲兵，无所陈之。使人复结绳而用之，甘其食，美其服，安其居，乐其俗。邻国相望，鸡犬之声相闻，民至老死，不相往来。

LXXX

In a little state with a small population, I would so order it, that, though there were individuals with the abilities of ten or a hundred men, there should be no employment of them; I would make the people, while looking on death as a grievous thing, yet not remove elsewhere (to avoid it).

Though they had boats and carriages, they should have no occasion to ride in them; though they had buff coats and sharp weapons, they should have no occasion to don or use them.

I would make the people return to the use of knotted cords (instead of the written characters).

They should think their (coarse) food sweet; their (plain) clothes beautiful; their (poor) dwellings places of rest; and their common (simple) ways sources of enjoyment.

There should be a neighbouring state within sight, and the voices of the fowls and dogs should be heard all the way from it to us, but I would make the people to old age, even to death, not have any intercourse with it.

SEAL SCRIPT

第八十一章

信言不美，美言不信。善者不辯，辯者不善。知者不博，博者不知。聖人不積，既以為人己愈有，既以與人己愈多。天之道，利而不害；聖人之道，為而不爭。

第八十一章

信言不美，美言不信。善者不辩，辩者不善。知者不博，博者不知。圣人不积，既以为人己愈有，既以与人己愈多。天之道，利而不害；圣人之道，为而不争。

LXXXI

Sincere words are not fine; fine words are not sincere. Those who are skilled (in the Tao) do not dispute (about it); the disputatious are not skilled in it. Those who know (the Tao) are not extensively learned; the extensively learned do not know it.

The sage does not accumulate (for himself). The more that he expends for others, the more does he possess of his own; the more that he gives to others, the more does he have himself.

With all the sharpness of the Way of Heaven, it injures not; with all the doing in the way of the sage he does not strive.

SEAL SCRIPT

DISCOVER MORE ANCIENT WISDOM

We invite you to explore the ultimate collection of Chinese military strategy:

"THE ART OF WAR" BY SUN TZU

ULTIMATE BILINGUAL EDITION (4-IN-1)

Master Sun's teachings on strategy, leadership, and victory are presented in their complete form, featuring:

- English
- Traditional Chinese
- Simplified Chinese
- Ancient Seal Script

This unique format allows you to compare different translations and witness the evolution of Chinese writing across millennia. Whether you're interested in military history, business strategy, leadership principles, or classical literature, Sun Tzu's timeless wisdom remains as relevant today as it was 2,500 years ago.

Find your copy at major online bookstores worldwide.

Stay tuned for our upcoming releases in the Ancient Classics Series, including other timeless works that have shaped Eastern philosophy and culture for generations.

www.ingramcontent.com/pod-product-compliance
Lightning Source LLC
Chambersburg PA
CBHW020255130626
46549CB00005B/2227